Bob Chilcott
Anthems 2

8 anthems for mixed voices

MUSIC DEPARTMENT

OXFORD
UNIVERSITY PRESS

OXFORD
UNIVERSITY PRESS

Great Clarendon Street, Oxford OX2 6DP, England
198 Madison Avenue, New York, NY 10016, USA

Oxford University Press is a department of the University of Oxford.
It furthers the University's aim of excellence in research, scholarship,
and education by publishing worldwide in

Oxford New York
Auckland Cape Town Hong Kong Karachi
Kuala Lumpur Madrid Melbourne Mexico City Nairobi
New Delhi Shanghai Taipei Toronto

With offices in

Argentina Austria Brazil Chile Czech Republic France Greece
Guatemala Hungary Italy Japan Poland Portugal Singapore
South Korea Switzerland Thailand Turkey Ukraine Vietnam

Oxford is a registered trade mark of Oxford University Press
in the UK and in certain other countries

10

ISBN 978-0-19-336493-6

Music and text origination by
Enigma Music Production Services, Amersham, Bucks.
Printed in Great Britain on acid-free paper by
Caligraving Ltd, Thetford, Norfolk.

Contents

A Thanksgiving   4

Dear Lord and Father of mankind   15

Love divine   27

Queen of the May   37

Let the earth acclaim him   44

The Lord's my Shepherd   46

The Lord's Prayer   53

This day   59

Composer's note

These eight pieces have been written over the past three years, and all but two are in print for the first time. Both 'The Lord's my Shepherd' and 'This day' were previously published with alternative scorings, and I have prepared new SATB versions for this collection.

I grew up singing the daily service of Evensong, first as a chorister and choral scholar in the Choir of King's College, Cambridge, and later as a temporary lay clerk in the Choir of Westminster Abbey and a freelance singer in many of the beautiful churches in London. It offered on a daily basis a time of reflection and quiet within the walls of some great buildings and spaces. The resonance of this aspect of my musical life has never gone away, and has deeply influenced my work as a composer, particularly in this collection of recent anthems.

I would like to thank Philip Croydon, Jane Griffiths, and Robyn Elton for their work on this publication.

*Generously commissioned by Jerry & Cathie Fischer, Ken & Penny Fischer,
and Jack & Linda Hoeschler for The King's Singers in celebration of their 40th Anniversary*

A Thanksgiving

St Richard of Chichester
(*c*.1197–1253)

BOB CHILCOTT

*This anthem is for unaccompanied double choir, but may also be performed by Choir 1 only, with organ accompaniment.

First performed by The King's Singers and the Choir of King's College, Cambridge, at King's College Chapel, on 1 May 2008.

for all the pains and in-sults which thou hast borne for us.

for all the pains and in-sults which thou hast borne for us.

for all the pains and in-sults which thou hast borne for us.

for all the pains and in-sults which thou hast borne for us.

thanks to

thanks be to

thanks

Commissioned to celebrate the 450th Anniversary of the foundation of Repton School

Dear Lord and Father of mankind

J. G. Whittier (1807–92)

BOB CHILCOTT

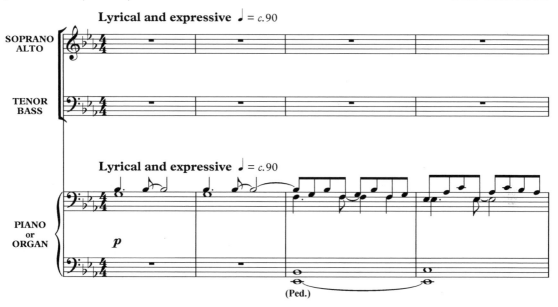

The optional congregation part that enters at bar 71 is the standard hymn tune 'Repton' by C. Hubert H. Parry (1848–1918).

First performed in Repton School Chapel on 26 May 2007, directed by John Bowley.

ser - vice find,_____ In deep- er, deep - er

re - verence praise.

In sim - ple   trust like theirs who heard, Be - side the

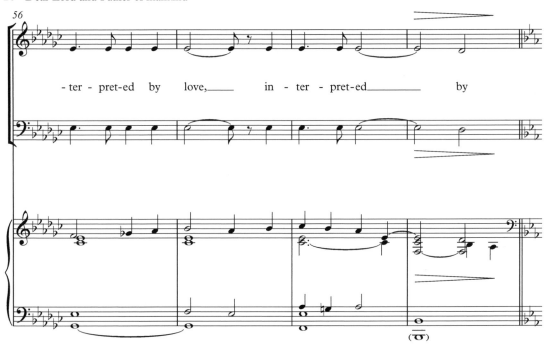

-ter - pret-ed by love,___ in - ter - pret-ed_____ by

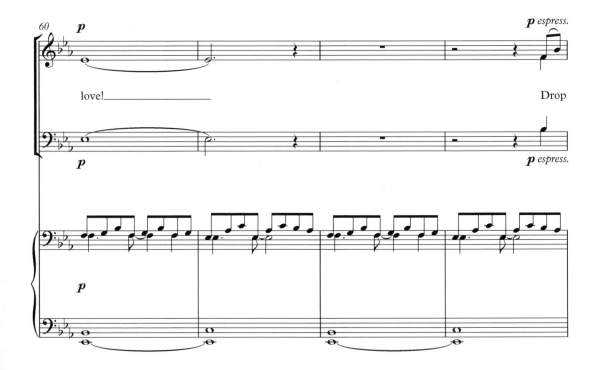

love!_____ Drop

*If not sung by the congregation, this part should be performed by a small group of singers from the main choir.

For - give,   for - give our   fool -   ish   ways!

The   beau - ty,   beau -   ty   of_____   thy   peace.

deep - er   re - verence praise,   in   deep - er   re - verence praise.

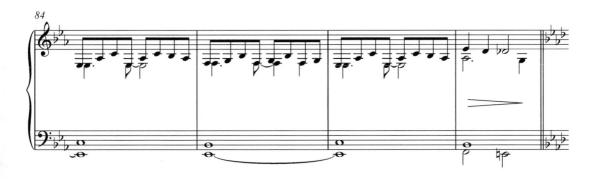

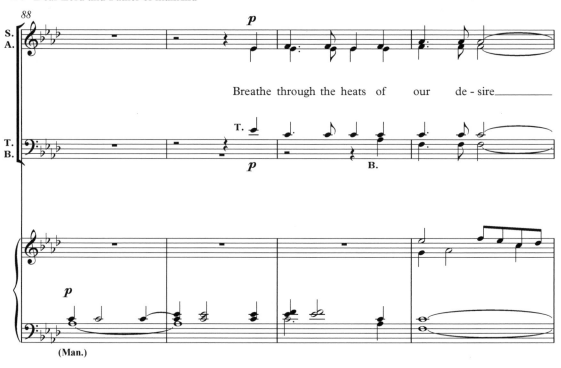

Breathe through the heats of our de - sire_____

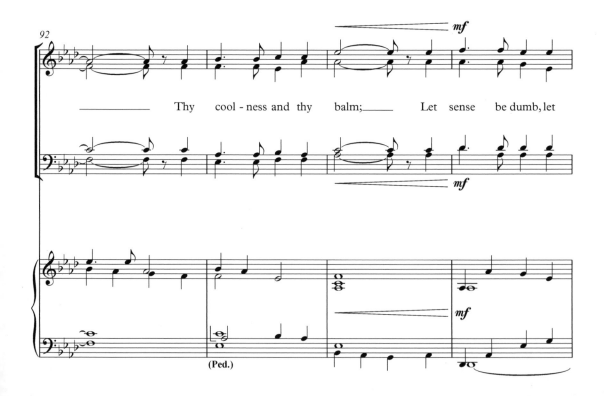

_____ Thy cool - ness and thy balm;_____ Let sense be dumb, let

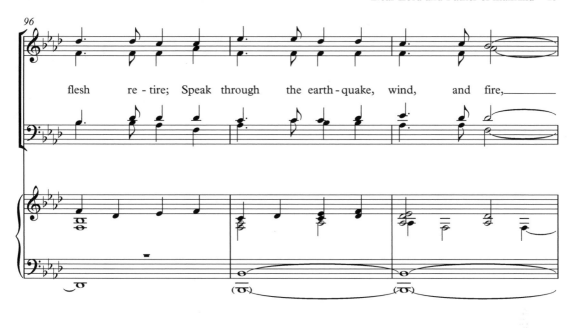

flesh re - tire; Speak through the earth-quake, wind, and fire,___

DESCANT
mp
Drop thy still dews of___ qui - et - ness,___

S. A.

O still small voice of calm,___ O

T. B.

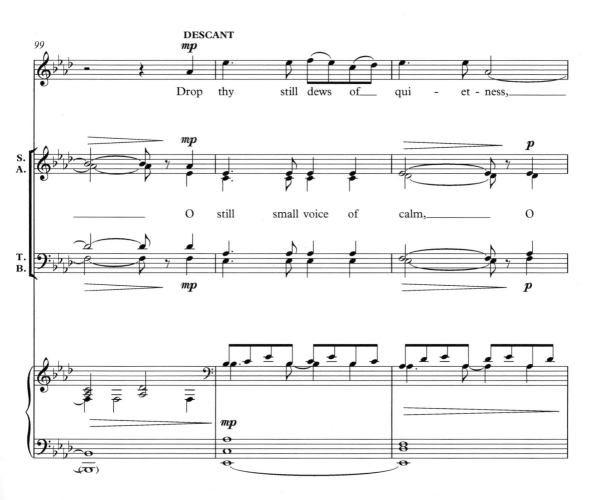

to Terry and Alyce Price; given with love and deep appreciation for them both on the occasion of their
tenth year in service at Preston Hollow Presbyterian Church, Dallas, TX;
and for the profound gift of their many decades of service to Christ and to His Church

Love divine

Charles Wesley (1707–88)

BOB CHILCOTT

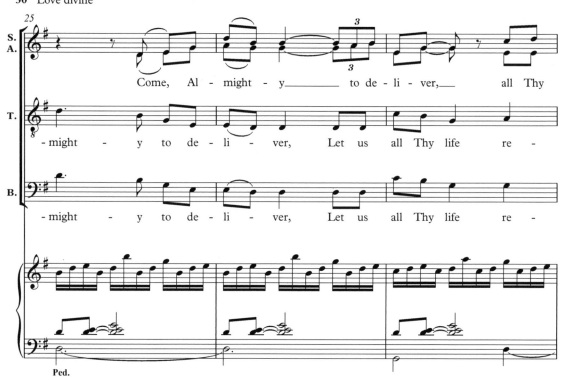

Come, Al - might - y_____ to de - li - ver,____ all Thy
- might - y to de - li - ver, Let us all Thy life re -
- might - y to de - li - ver, Let us all Thy life re -

life re - ceive;_____ Sud - den - ly re - turn, and
- ceive, all Thy life____ re - ceive; Sud - den -
- ceive,_____ all Thy life re - ceive;

for the marriage of Jonna and Quinn

Queen of the May

Trad. 19th cent.

BOB CHILCOTT

*The percussion part may be played on any appropriate instrument, e.g. handbells, crotales, chime bars, or triangles.

blos - soms to - day, O Queen of the An - gels and Queen of the

May.   O Ma - ry, we   crown thee with   blos-soms to - day,   O

May.   O Ma - ry, we   crown thee with   blos-soms to - day,   O

Queen   of   the   An - gels   and   Queen   of   the   May._____

Queen   of   the   An - gels   and   Queen   of   the   May._____

Ma - ry,   we   crown_ thee with blos - soms to - day,   O

Ma - ry,   we   crown thee with blos - soms to - day,   O

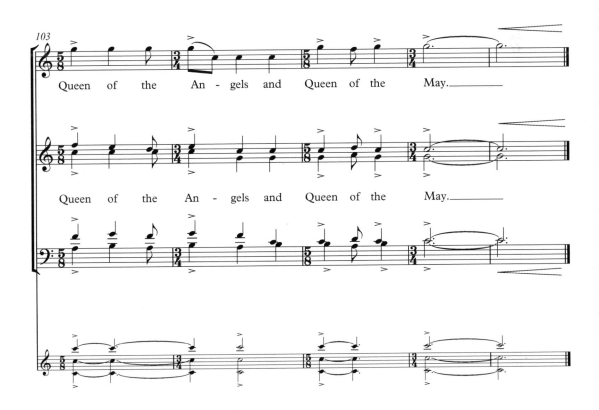

Queen   of   the   An - gels and   Queen of the   May._____

Queen   of   the   An - gels and   Queen of the   May._____

for Ashley Grote and The St Cecilia Singers on the occasion of their 60th anniversary

Let the earth acclaim him

Timothy Dudley-Smith
(b. 1926)

BOB CHILCOTT

46

to Neil and Kristen on the occasion of their marriage, 5 May 2007

The Lord's my Shepherd

Psalm 23
The Scottish Psalter, 1650

BOB CHILCOTT

First published in Bullard (ed.), *The Oxford Book of Flexible Anthems* (ISBN 978–0–19–335895–9) in an arrangement for unison voices, SA, or SA Men.

for Becky

The Lord's Prayer

BOB CHILCOTT

13

us this___ day___ our_ dai - ly___ bread;___ And for-

17

-give us our tres-pas-ses, As we for-give them that tres - pass a-

20

mp cresc.

-gainst us; And lead us not in-to temp - ta - tion, But de - li - ver us from

B. *mp cresc.*

mp cresc.

for the Crescent City Choral Festival, New Orleans, and Cheryl Dupont, Director

This day

Jewish text
adap. Bob Chilcott

BOB CHILCOTT

An accompaniment for strings and harp is available to hire from the publisher's Hire Library or appropriate agent.

First published as part of the larger work, *This Day* (ISBN 978–0–19–335933–8), scored for SA and piano.

This day— in-scribe us for a hap-py, hap-py life.————————

S. This day hear our cry.———————— This day ac - cept our prayer in

A. This day hear our cry.———————— This day———— ac -

T. This day hear our cry.———————— This day ac -

B. This day hear our cry.———————— This day, this—

13

mer - cy and fa-vour, This day sup-port us with your right - eous hand.

- cept our prayer with fa - vour,___ and with your right - eous. hand.___

- cept our_ prayer with fa - vour, with your right - eous. hand.___

day,_____ this_ day, This day, with your right - eous. hand.

16

f   *mf dim.*

This day ac-cept our prayer in mer - cy and fa-vour, This day,_____ this_

f   *mf dim.*

This day,_____ this day,_____ This day,_____ this

f   *mf dim.*

This day,_____ this day,_____ This day,_____ this

f   *mf dim.*

This day,_____ this day,_____ This day,_____ this

f   *mf dim.*